ENERGY FOR THE FUTURE
ENERGY FROM THE EARTH

by Susan Wroble

FOCUS READERS
NAVIGATOR

WWW.FOCUSREADERS.COM

Focus Readers is distributed by North Star Editions:
sales@northstareditions.com | 888-417-0195

Produced for Focus Readers by Red Line Editorial.

Content Consultant: Ken Wisian, PhD, Bureau of Economic Geology, Jackson School of Geosciences, University of Texas at Austin

Photographs ©: Shutterstock Images, cover, 1, 4–5, 7, 8–9, 11, 13, 14–15, 17, 19, 20–21, 22, 24, 26–27, 29

Library of Congress Cataloging-in-Publication Data
Names: Wroble, Susan, author.
Title: Energy from the Earth / Susan Wroble.
Description: Lake Elmo, MN : Focus Readers, 2022. | Series: Energy for the future | Includes index. | Audience: Grades 4-6
Identifiers: LCCN 2021035795 (print) | LCCN 2021035796 (ebook) | ISBN 9781637390580 (hardcover) | ISBN 9781637391129 (paperback) | ISBN 9781637391662 (ebook) | ISBN 9781637392157 (pdf)
Subjects: LCSH: Geothermal engineering--Juvenile literature.
Classification: LCC TJ280.7 .W76 2022 (print) | LCC TJ280.7 (ebook) | DDC 621.44--dc23
LC record available at https://lccn.loc.gov/2021035795
LC ebook record available at https://lccn.loc.gov/2021035796

Printed in the United States of America
Mankato, MN
012022

ABOUT THE AUTHOR

Susan Wroble is a children's writer with a passion for science, education, and dogs. She has degrees in electrical engineering and foreign affairs. When she isn't writing, you can find her working with her husband and their therapy dogs in Denver, Colorado.

TABLE OF CONTENTS

CHAPTER 1

Technology in Action 5

CHAPTER 2

History of Geothermal Energy 9

THAT'S AMAZING!

Land of Fire and Ice 12

CHAPTER 3

How Geothermal Energy Works 15

CHAPTER 4

Benefits and Problems 21

CHAPTER 5

The Future of the Technology 27

Focus on Energy from the Earth • 30
Glossary • 31
To Learn More • 32
Index • 32

TECHNOLOGY IN ACTION

In a broad valley in southwestern Utah, sagebrush dots the land. There are few trees. The nearest town of Milford lies 10 miles (16 km) away. Fewer than 2,000 people live there. The desert valley seems like the middle of nowhere. Yet this place is special. It may hold the keys to a cleaner future.

Most of Earth's heat is deep underground. But in places such as Yellowstone National Park, the heat reaches Earth's surface.

This desert is home to a project called FORGE. FORGE stands for Frontier Observatory for Research in Geothermal Energy. Geothermal energy is energy within our planet. Earth's center is hot. The core is hotter than the surface of the sun. In some places on Earth's surface, boiling water or steam gushes out of the ground. Elsewhere, volcanoes spew hot lava. In all these places, Earth's heat is close to the surface. People can reach it easily. But in most places, the heat lies far underground. The challenge is reaching it.

The FORGE project uses new tools and ideas. For example, engineers test new ways of drilling. Scientists try new ways

Earth's heat has 50,000 times more energy than the energy held by all the world's oil and gas.

of mapping underground heat. The goal is to make geothermal energy **accessible**. That way, more people could use Earth's heat directly. They could also convert that heat into electricity.

Geothermal energy has many benefits. It is clean. It can be used at any time. And the energy is **renewable**. All of that is good for the planet.

CHAPTER 2

HISTORY OF GEOTHERMAL ENERGY

People have been using Earth's energy for thousands of years. In North America, ancient Indigenous peoples settled near hot springs. The ancient Chinese built palaces above naturally heated pools. The ancient Romans built temples at hot springs.

In the first century CE, the Romans built a temple and bathhouse in what is now Bath, England.

Later, people used Earth's energy to heat larger areas. A village in France used a system of pipes in the 1300s. The pipes carried water from a local hot spring. They delivered the hot water to homes. Over time, other countries developed their own heating systems.

HEAT FROM THE EARTH

Earth is made up of layers. The inner core reaches up to 10,800 degrees Fahrenheit (6,000°C). The mantle is mostly solid rock. The outer crust is in pieces called tectonic plates. These huge rocky sheets contain whole continents. Earth's heat reaches the surface where plates meet or separate. It also reaches the surface where the crust is thin.

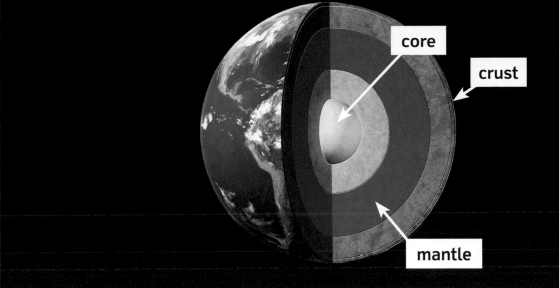

The outer crust that people live on makes up only a tiny layer of Earth.

In 1904, an Italian prince had a chemical factory heated by steam. He thought the steam could be used to make electricity. So, the prince experimented. He used the steam to power a **generator**. It lit five light bulbs. By 1908, the prince had built the first geothermal power plant. By 2021, nearly 30 countries had geothermal power plants.

LAND OF FIRE AND ICE

Iceland used to be one of the poorest countries in Europe. It relied on coal and oil from other countries for energy. Getting these **fossil fuels** was expensive. The fuels also polluted the country. Black smoke blanketed the capital.

In the 1970s, oil prices rose. Instead of paying those prices, Iceland looked at its natural resources. Iceland has more than 200 volcanoes. The country sits on the line between two tectonic plates. These plates are slowly pulling apart. Heat rises to the surface.

Iceland is rich in geothermal energy. So, the people started piping steam to heat buildings. They built geothermal power plants to provide electricity. Energy costs went down. Pollution

Hverir, Iceland, has many natural steam vents and hot springs.

went down, too. Now, more than half of Iceland's homes use clean geothermal energy.

Iceland has become a world leader in renewable energy. It's using that knowledge to help East Africa harness geothermal energy. Countries there sit on a tectonic plate that is splitting apart.

CHAPTER 3

HOW GEOTHERMAL ENERGY WORKS

There are three methods of using geothermal energy. They are electricity, direct heat, and heat pumps. In some areas, wells reach hot steam. This steam is hot enough to generate electricity. To do so, the steam powers a wheel-like turbine. It causes the turbine to turn. The turbine spins a generator.

The Philippines (shown) and Indonesia are two of the world's top producers of geothermal energy.

The generator turns that energy of motion into electricity. Meanwhile, the original steam is cooled and turned back into water. It is sent back underground. There, the water heats up and becomes steam. The whole cycle repeats.

In other areas, drilling reaches slightly cooler water or steam. In this case, producing electricity is not as **efficient**. So, people use the geothermal energy for direct heat. Pipes carry the hot water or steam. The pipes provide hot water to homes and businesses. They also warm the air to heat buildings. Sometimes this geothermal energy can heat a whole town.

Nearly every place can use heat pumps. The pumps do not rely on hot water or steam underground. Instead, they depend

GEOTHERMAL ELECTRICITY GENERATION

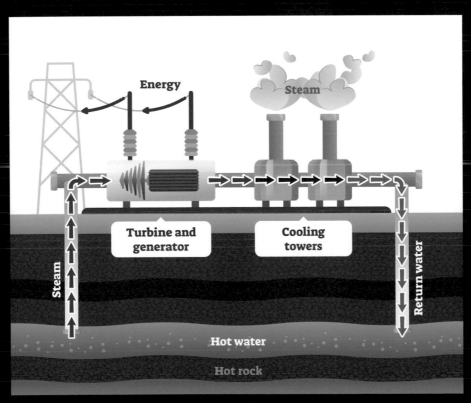

Energy

Steam

Turbine and generator

Cooling towers

Steam

Return water

Hot water

Hot rock

on soil temperature. On the surface, the ground's temperature changes with the weather. But at approximately 3 to 10 feet (0.9–3.0 m) deep, the soil temperature is more constant.

To use heat pumps, people bury pipes with liquid in them. The pipes may be

THE GEYSERS

A geyser is hot water shooting up from the earth. A fumarole is hot steam rising from the earth. In 1847, William Elliott confused the two. While hunting in California, he found a steamy canyon. He called it the Geysers. The name was wrong, but it stuck. Now the area is home to the world's largest group of geothermal power plants. There are 13 plants. They supply enough power for a small city.

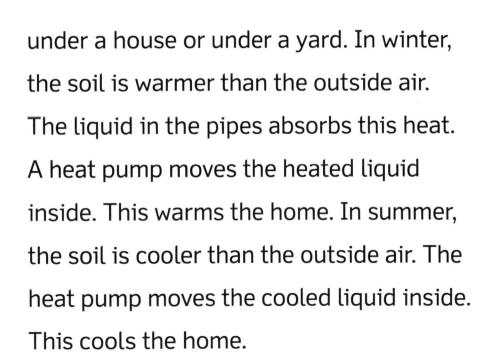

Iceland's Blue Lagoon is an example of direct heat.
Visitors can relax in the naturally heated pool.

under a house or under a yard. In winter,
the soil is warmer than the outside air.
The liquid in the pipes absorbs this heat.
A heat pump moves the heated liquid
inside. This warms the home. In summer,
the soil is cooler than the outside air. The
heat pump moves the cooled liquid inside.
This cools the home.

CHAPTER 4

BENEFITS AND PROBLEMS

Most of the energy people use comes from fossil fuels. These fuels include coal, oil, and natural gas. Fossil fuels have two main problems. First, they are running out. Second, burning them releases greenhouse gases. These gases trap heat in Earth's atmosphere, causing **climate change**. Other energy sources,

Coal power plants release greenhouse gases into the atmosphere and contribute to the climate crisis.

Volcanoes are openings in Earth's crust. Hot gases and magma from deep within Earth sometimes spew out.

such as sunlight and wind, are renewable and clean. But solar energy depends on the sun shining. And wind power only works when the wind blows.

In contrast, Earth is always giving off heat. Some heat comes from the planet's creation more than four billion years ago. Some comes from **elements** decaying inside Earth. These elements break down into other elements over time, releasing heat. Earth will keep producing heat for billions of years. There is enough heat to supply all the energy humans could need.

Also, geothermal energy is clean. Geothermal plants are small. They produce few or no greenhouse gases. By switching to geothermal power, people can slow climate change.

Geothermal power does have some challenges. At first, it can be costly. Drilling is expensive. But once plants are built, costs are low. Also, older models of geothermal wells must be able to reach hot **fluids**. Finding underground

 Workers manage a geothermal power plant in Indonesia.

reservoirs of hot fluids is not easy. In some places, reservoirs don't exist.

Early geothermal plants had another problem. They pulled up fluid from deep within the earth. But they did not replace the fluid. So, the land caved in. Scientists worked to solve this problem. Now, geothermal plants refill the underground reservoirs. The land remains stable.

Scientists are learning how best to harness Earth's energy. They are working to solve problems of cost and underground mapping. And they are developing new technologies so people everywhere can replace fossil fuels with geothermal energy.

UNDERGROUND SPONGES

Aboveground, water may flow in rivers. It may collect in lakes. But underground, water and steam move through spaces in the rocks. These spaces can act like tiny sponges, soaking up the fluids. As fluids flow through the spaces, they heat up. Fluid, heat, and flow to Earth's surface are all needed to produce geothermal power.

CHAPTER 5

THE FUTURE OF THE TECHNOLOGY

As of 2021, nearly 40 countries could get all their electricity from geothermal energy. Many of them are along the Ring of Fire. But new technologies could let people access Earth's heat anywhere. One technology is the Enhanced Geothermal System. Water is pumped underground to crack

The Ring of Fire surrounds the Pacific Ocean. The ring contains most of Earth's active volcanoes.

rocks. This creates a new reservoir. Water flows among the rocks and collects heat. Pumps bring the hot water to the surface to create electricity. Then pumps send the water back underground to collect more heat. The cycle repeats.

Another technology is the Closed Loop Geothermal System (CLGS). A CLGS works likes a heat pump. But it reaches down to much hotter temperatures. Fluid-filled pipes are placed deep underground. No reservoir is needed. The rocks heat the water as it flows by.

Geothermal technologies will keep improving. As they do, prices will come down. More people will switch to geothermal energy. This move will help slow climate change. Geothermal energy is part of the world's future.

CLOSED LOOP GEOTHERMAL

A CLGS removes the risk of earthquakes, groundwater pollution, and greenhouse gas emissions.

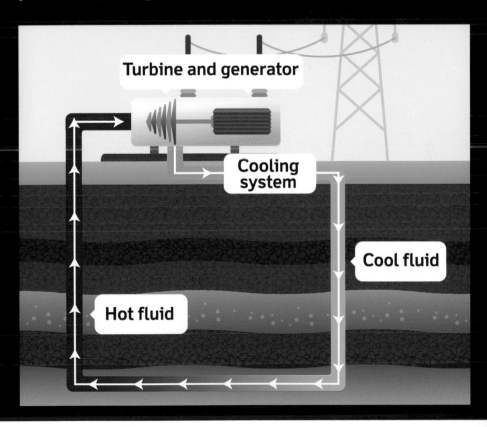

Turbine and generator

Cooling system

Cool fluid

Hot fluid

FOCUS ON
ENERGY FROM
THE EARTH

Write your answers on a separate piece of paper.

1. Write a paragraph summarizing the three ways of using geothermal energy.

2. Which geothermal technology do you find most interesting? Why?

3. What do heat pumps depend on?

   A. underground reservoirs
   B. geysers
   C. soil temperature

4. How might a CLGS be helpful in slowing climate change?

   A. The technology could be used anywhere, allowing more people to stop using fossil fuels.
   B. The technology causes more earthquakes, stopping people from using energy.
   C. The technology creates more greenhouse gases than other technologies.

Answer key on page 32.

GLOSSARY

accessible
Able to be reached or used.

climate change
A human-caused global crisis involving long-term changes in Earth's temperature and weather patterns.

efficient
Accomplishing as much as possible with as little effort or as few resources as possible.

elements
Pure substances. Each is made of only one kind of atom.

fluids
Substances, such as liquids or gases, that have no fixed shape and can flow.

fossil fuels
Energy sources that come from the remains of plants and animals that died long ago.

generator
A machine that turns the energy of motion into electricity.

renewable
Having to do with natural resources that never run out.

reservoirs
Places where fluids collect.

TO LEARN MORE

BOOKS

Bard, Mariel. *Geothermal Energy: Harnessing the Power of Earth's Heat*. New York: PowerKids Press, 2018.

Brearley, Laurie. *Geothermal Energy: The Energy Inside Our Planet*. New York: Scholastic, 2019.

Eboch, M. M. *Geothermal Energy*. North Mankato, MN: Capstone Press, 2019.

NOTE TO EDUCATORS

Visit **www.focusreaders.com** to find lesson plans, activities, links, and other resources related to this title.

INDEX

climate change, 21, 23, 29

Closed Loop Geothermal System (CLGS), 28–29

direct heat, 7, 15–16

drilling, 6, 16, 23

electricity, 7, 11, 12, 15–17, 27–28

Enhanced Geothermal System, 27–28

fluids, 23–25, 28–29

fossil fuels, 12, 21, 25

Frontier Observatory for Research in Geothermal Energy (FORGE), 6

generator, 11, 15–17, 29

geothermal power plants, 11, 12, 18, 23–24

greenhouse gases, 21, 23, 29

heat pumps, 15, 17–19, 28

Iceland, 12–13

steam, 6, 11, 12, 15–18, 25

tectonic plates, 10, 12–13

turbine, 15, 17, 29

Answer Key: **1.** Answers will vary; **2.** Answers will vary; **3.** C; **4.** A